*This book was purchased
with funds from a
generous donation by*

Dr. Kathryn W. Davis

LOIS LOWRY

DEBORAH GRAHAME-SMITH

Cavendish Square

New York

Published in 2014 by Cavendish Square Publishing, LLC
303 Park Avenue South, Suite 1247, New York, NY 10010

Library of Congress Cataloging-in-Publication Data
Grahame-Smith, Deborah.
Lois Lowry / Deborah Grahame-Smith.
pages cm. — (Spotlight on children's authors)
Includes bibliographical references and index.
ISBN 978-1-62712-274-0 (hardcover) ISBN 978-1-62712-275-7 (paperback) ISBN 978-1-62712-276-4 (ebook)
1. Lowry, Lois—Juvenile literature. 2. Authors, American—20th century—Biography—Juvenile literature. 3. Children's stories—Authorship—Juvenile literature. I. Title.

PS3562.O923Z75 2014
813'.54—dc23

2013030146

Editorial Director: Dean Miller
Senior Editor: Peter Mavrikis
Copy Editor: Cynthia Roby
Art Director: Jeffrey Talbot
Designer: Amy Greenan
Production Manager: Jennifer Ryder-Talbot
Production Editor: Andrew Coddington
Photo research by Julie Alissi, J8 Media

Cover photo courtesy of Lois Lowry.

The photographs in this book with permission and through courtesy of: courtesy of Lois Lowry, 4, 6, 10, 14, 21, 24, 27, 28, 32, 36; © Jan Nagle, 9, 13, 16, 18, 22; Kevin Winter/Staff/Getty Images Entertainment/Getty Images, 35.

Printed in the United States of America

CONTENTS

INTRODUCTION:

A Far-Out Profession

A snowy afternoon in early January may not have been the best time to board a flight from Boston to New York. But just that morning Lois Lowry had received a phone call and learned that she had won the 1990 Newbery Medal for her novel *Number the Stars*. The Newbery committee asked Lois to appear on the *Today* show the following morning. Heavy snowflakes or not, the excitement of the news may have allowed Lois to slip temporarily into a foggy but pleasant mental state.

The Pan Am shuttle should have taken about one hour to fly from Logan Airport in Boston to New York, putting Lois snugly at her hotel by about 7:00 PM. Instead, her plane circled La Guardia Airport until it ran low on fuel close to midnight and was forced to land in upstate New York to refuel and wait out the storm. Lois did not reach her hotel until 2:00 AM.

Of course, the *Today* show is a bright-and-early broadcast so she was in a car sent by the studio at 6:30 AM. Once on set she began to fuel her weary brain with plenty of coffee, waiting with her fellow interviewees in the Green Room. Lois noticed a white card on a bulletin board describing herself and another guest on the show, fellow author Ed Young: 2 KIDS BOOKS PEOPLE.

The night's flying machine events continued into the day, but now instead of an airplane, the drama involved a space shuttle. *Today* show producers learned that the shuttle *Columbia* had been cleared that morning by NASA for takeoff. In the fluid environment that is live TV, breaking news events like shuttle launches often push scheduled personalities off the morning-show radar. Lois taped an interview that was shown later in other time zones. In four years time, Lois would receive another Newbery Medal, for *The Giver*, presumably with more media opportunities and fewer mishaps.

In her Newbery Medal acceptance speech for *Number the Stars* Lois recounted her *Today* show experience and also mentioned that she carries in her wallet a message she received years earlier in a Chinese fortune cookie: "You will be rich and famous in a far-out profession." She believes that the fortune came true the night that she accepted the award and acknowledges that the true riches of her writing career are the "importance of human connection" she shares with her readers and with all of the professional people— writers, agents, editors, illustrators, and librarians—who bring great books, far-out and otherwise, to children everywhere.

Lois at age one with mother and sister living in Hawaii.

Chapter 1
BORN IN THE MIDDLE

Lois Ann Hammersberg was born in Honolulu, Hawaii, on March 20, 1937. Hawaii was not yet a state, so her birth certificate lists the location as the Territory of Hawaii. Her father, Robert (Bob), was an Army major who would later be deployed overseas during World War II. Her mother, Katherine (Kate) taught kindergarten. The names Lois and Ann were given in honor of her two aunts. Originally she was to be called Cena after her Norwegian grandmother, but that grandmother insisted that an American baby should have an American name.

Her older sister, Helen, was born three years earlier, in February 1934. Her younger brother, Jon, would be born almost six years later, in January 1943. That left Lois "right smack in the middle," as her character Gooney Bird Greene would one day claim as her preferred position in the classroom, and in life. Lois's birth order in the family suited her, since she craved solitude and enjoyed being left alone to nurture her imagination. Photos of Lois as a small child show an intensity and curiosity that pass over her cherubic face like fair-weather clouds floating across a sunny sky.

Lois's mother, Kate, introduced the classics such as *Alice's Adventures in Wonderland* and *Winnie the Pooh*, and made sure the Hammersberg children made frequent trips to the town library. Big sister Helen also read to Lois, who became a reader herself at the precocious age of three. Lois remembers her grandfather reading aloud to the family after dinner, cozy around the hearth in their Carlisle, Pennsylvania, home. Lois lived with her grandparents while her father was stationed in the Pacific during the war. It was a spacious and comfortable house in a small college town, "with little picket fences and puppies," she recalls. She completed elementary school there. Lois Lensky's *Strawberry Girl* was a favorite of Lois's during this time. Later she would be amused at the tendency of some readers to confuse her with the other Lois L.

One evening at a dinner party Lois's grandfather brought her by the hand into the living room to recite a long poem she had memorized, for the entertainment of their guests. "It was kind of a bizarre thing for a child who weighed about 22 pounds to be able to say this multi-paged poem," she later told an interviewer. Standing in her footed pajamas Lois recited "Thanatopsis" by William Cullen Bryant. Many years later, a wealthy guest at that dinner party bequeathed a small part of his estate to the little girl who had apparently impressed and charmed him with her recitation. One half of one percent sounds like small change, but it was enough money for Lois to buy a blue Pontiac, which she drove to California after leaving college.

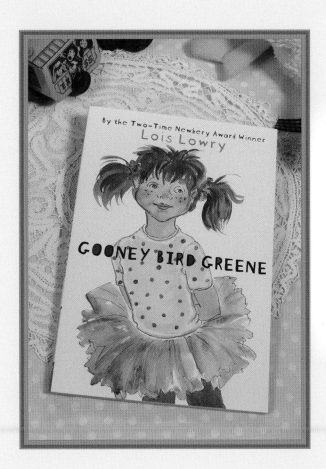

RIGHT SMACK IN THE MIDDLE OF EVERYTHING

In 2002 Lois began a series of books about rambunctious second-grader Gooney Bird Greene, who wears outrageous outfits to school (cowboy boots and pajamas) and loves to have her desk smack in the middle of the classroom. "She's exactly the kind of child I was not," Lois says. "I was always the one who sat silently with my head down looking at the floor. And I was terribly shy. So she falls into the category of the kind of child I yearned to be."

But before that adventure, Lois and her family would embark on a journey across the globe to join her father after the war ended. Tokyo was a long way from Carlisle's puppies and picket fences. In fact, it was "Elsewhere" from anywhere she had known.

Lois at age 17 dressed
for her high school
graduation.

Chapter 2
FINDING ELSEWHERE

When Lois was eleven years old she moved to Japan with her mother and siblings. They joined her father in Tokyo and lived in a small section of the city that had been Americanized for military families. It was called Washington Heights, and it was designed to make families feel comfortable while living so far from home.

Lois described the experience, vividly in the present tense, in her 1994 Newbery Award acceptance speech for *The Giver*. "We live in an American-style house, with American neighbors, and our little community has its own movie theater, which shows American movies; and a small church, a tiny library, and an elementary school. In many ways it is an odd replica of a United States village." There was no practical reason to venture into the Japanese culture, no way to feel uncomfortable or unsafe in a strange land.

But Lois sensed the "Elsewhere" of the exotic environment that surrounded her. As a shy but curious young person, she was drawn to explore the unfamiliar sights and sounds that she was shielded from by her small, safe world. Many times, without telling her parents, she rode her bicycle outside the fenced-in American community, down a hill and into a pungent part of Tokyo called Shibuya. She explored Shibuya regularly and soaked up the otherness of its vibrant people and shops. Lois was feeling almost invisible until one day when someone approached her as she stood on a street corner.

A woman touched Lois's hair and said something in Japanese that she could not quite understand. "*Kirai-des*," I dislike you. Had she done something wrong? If only her Japanese were better! Then Lois realized that the woman had told her "*Kirei-des*," you are pretty. Before Lois could smile a thank you, the woman disappeared. This magical moment of instant connection out of disconnection haunted her.

Lois and her family stayed in Japan from 1948 to 1950. Her experience there was mostly positive. Even though the curriculum at the American school did not inspire or challenge her, the lessons on the Technicolor streets of Shibuya had fed her creative spirit in ways no classroom in the world ever could.

OPENING THE GATE

Like Lois in Tokyo, her character Jonas in *The Giver* is an eleven-year-old child (on the cusp of twelve) who lives in a world designed to be safe and homogenous. In a society without color, there is no discrimination. With no money, the crime of theft does not exist. Everything on the surface looks wonderful. But just as the comfortable American world of Washington Heights in Tokyo left young Lois unsatisfied, Jonas longs for what is real—even if there is a risk in the discovery of what lies "Elsewhere." In her Newbery Award acceptance speech, Lois said, "The man that I named the Giver passed along to the boy knowledge, history, memories, color, pain, laughter, love, and truth. Every time you place a book in the hands of a child, you do the same thing. It is very risky. But each time a child opens a book, he pushes open the gate that separates him from Elsewhere."

Lois at age 19 in her wedding photo.

Chapter 3
COLLEGE, MARRIAGE, AND COLLEGE

Lois traveled back to the United States in 1950 and hopscotched schools after returning to Carlisle, Pennsylvania. During her adolescent years she wrote stories and poems faithfully in her notebook. At thirteen the young, solitary writer received a typewriter from her parents. In 1951 she moved to Governor's Island, New York, to attend Curtis High School on Staten Island, and in 1952 she continued high school at Brooklyn's Parker Collegiate Institute. In high school Lois won writing awards and a scholarship that helped her to pay for college.

As a freshman at Brown University in Rhode Island, Lois wore the college uniform of the time: loafers and knee socks, plaid skirts and cashmere sweaters. She was a studious participant in the writing program and enjoyed university life. Then in her sophomore year, she met a football player who was also a student at Brown, two years her senior. Lois married that athlete, Donald Grey Lowry, in 1956, and they made their first home in San Diego, California.

Donald was a naval officer and so, just as her family had done, Lois moved around frequently as the children arrived. She gave

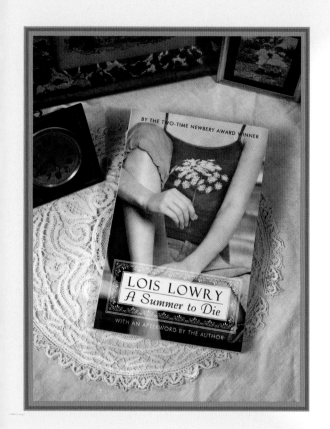

FIRST BOOKS FOR KIDS

Reviews and reactions to her first novel, *A Summer to Die*, encouraged Lois to focus on writing for kids. "When you write for kids," she told an interviewer, "you are writing for people who can still be affected by what you write in ways that might change them. When you write for adults, they can be affected by what you've written but they're already well molded and shaped. It's kids who are still in the process of growth and change and it's why I think I take very seriously what I do because it does affect kids that way."

birth to two boys and two girls by the time she was twenty-six years old. In 1962, Lois's older sister, Helen, died of cancer at the age of twenty-eight. This occurred while Lois was in the midst of young motherhood and new life, and her grief would later be the catalyst for writing her first novel, *A Summer to Die*.

Cambridge, Massachusetts, became home when Donald entered law school at Harvard. Then the family settled in Maine, and when their youngest child entered kindergarten, Lois resumed her studies, earning a degree in English literature from the University of Southern Maine in 1972. She then began graduate work. Lois discovered a talent for photography in grad school and later incorporated this passion into her writing career. She saw the gap in her college studies as a possibly necessary event in her life. "My children grew up in Maine," she says. "So did I."

"I was young when I went to college. I had just turned seventeen and I was immature as proven by rushing off to get married. That's an immature thing to do. So when I went back, and was by then grown, I took it all more seriously. I studied harder, I learned more, I cared more. So I guess in a way I don't regret having interrupted my education, though I would not advise young people to do it."

After graduation, Lois began a longed-for profession as a freelance journalist and photographer, writing for magazines such as *Redbook*. After seeing a few of her pieces, an editor at that magazine encouraged her to write a book for children. As this part of her life flourished, Lois and her husband grew apart, and they divorced in 1977, the year *A Summer to Die* was published. Lois described her first novel as "a highly fictionalized retelling" of her sister Helen's death. Lois turned forty that year.

Fourth grade brought
Anastasia a full plate of
problems, from a pink wart
on her thumb to a new and
"unnecessary" baby brother.

Chapter 4
THE WRITING LIFE

A year after *A Summer to Die* was published, Lois wrote her second novel, *Find a Stranger, Say Goodbye*, tackling another sensitive topic: an adopted teenager's quest to find her "real" parents. The book got mixed reviews but established Lois as an author who handled difficult subjects in "topical novels" deftly.

Switching gears, she created a quirky new character, Anastasia Krupnik, a bespectacled ten-year-old girl with Hubbard squash-colored hair, a nose sprinkled with exactly fourteen freckles, and "seven others in places that she preferred people not to know about." The first Anastasia book was introduced in 1979, and eight more titles followed. Eventually Lowry wrote another series that focused on the adventures of Anastasia's younger brother, Sam.

Then Lois created another young character, Annemarie Johansen, who lived in Copenhagen, Denmark, during the Holocaust. *Number the Stars* tells the story of Annemarie's and her Danish family's bravery during World War II, when an entire country mobilized silently to save their Jewish citizens from the Nazi's death camps. Based on real people and events, Lois's novel was celebrated by

Horn Book as "seamless, compelling, and memorable." With this novel, Lois crossed the threshold of celebrity, becoming a household name in the world of children's authors as the last decade of the twentieth century began.

JUST A FEW LINES FROM *BABAR*

After her divorce in 1977, Lois was busy as a writer and a self-described hermit. She went on dates but explains in her autobiography that, "Having dates is sort of fun when you are fifteen or seventeen or nineteen, but when you are forty, it is not fun." Then a man named Martin—actually her car insurance agent—called her on the phone and asked her to meet him for coffee. She grumpily agreed. Maybe he would raise her rates if she refused? During their date Martin responded to a suggestion Lois made by quoting a line from the *Babar* books: "You have good ideas, Cornelius. When I am king I will give you a green hat." This remark seemed odd to Lois, yet also intriguing. Still searching for a graceful exit she told him thanks, but, she preferred men with facial hair, like the singer Willie Nelson. When Martin grew a beard to impress her, she took a second look at this insurance man, and they went on to share thirty fulfilling years together.

Lois and Martin skiing (opposite).

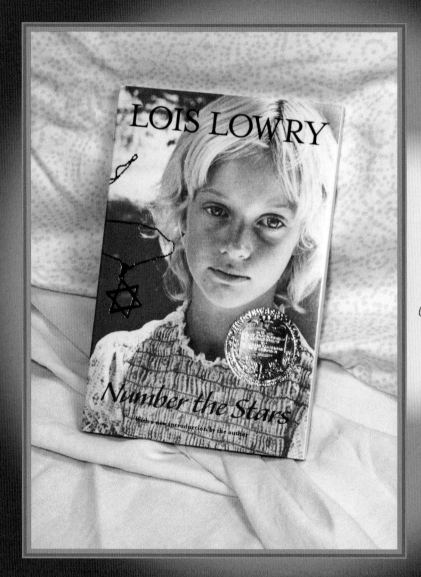

LOIS LOWRY

Number the Stars

With a new introduction by the author

Annemarie
Johansen
dealt with the
fear of Nazi
Germany during
World War II.

Chapter 5
HIGH SHINY BOOTS AND A STRANGE APPLE

The idea for the novel *Number the Stars* began with a friendship across cultures and continents. Lois met Annelise, a Danish woman who was living in the States. During their talks and travels together, the women shared memories of their childhoods during World War II. The character Annemarie Johansen evolved from the stories Annelise told Lois. Many of Annelise's memories were comprised of small moments in a child's consciousness: mittens worn to bed on a cold night; the "high shiny boots" worn by the Nazi soldiers who occupied Copenhagen in 1943. Lois mentioned these boots throughout the book to display the fear felt by children living in occupied Denmark. Her longtime editor at Houghton Mifflin, Walter Lorraine, flagged this repetition as a possible problem. Lois respected and valued his opinion as ever, but asked for time to think about it.

Then, while on a book publicity tour, Lois met a Holocaust survivor living in Australia who had a childhood memory as a toddler of watching her mother being taken away by the Nazis. All she remembered years later was the high shiny boots, exactly as

THE *NUMBER THE STARS* MOVIE PROJECT

Actor Sean Astin, who played Samwise in the *Lord of the Rings* films and also Mikey in the 80s Steven Spielberg classic, *The Goonies*, has been working quietly and tirelessly to see Lois's novel brought to the big screen. He and Lois corresponded for a while and then met in 2011 at the Getty Center in Los Angeles to discuss the project. Lois observed how the actor handled his fame with grace and was friendly to fans who recognized him during the visit. "Sean and his wife [Christine] have written a wonderful script that is quite true to the book; they have spent time in Denmark doing research, and have made all of the preparations for the film . . . all but the money-raising! And now they are hard at work on that."

Lois with Sean Astin.

Sean, who also directs and produces movies, calls this his "passion project" and is determined to raise the funds he needs first, before hiring actors and moving ahead on the production. "I am willing to fail and do it this way," Sean says, "rather than compromise my integrity."

described to Lois by Annelise. So when Lois returned to the States and responded to her editor, she asked that all of the references to the boots remain, even if it seemed that there were too many. "I decided that if any reviewer should call attention to the overuse of that image—none ever has—I would simply tell them that those high shiny boots had trampled on several million childhoods and I was sorry I hadn't several million more pages on which to mention that."

Lois's second Newbery Medal–winner, *The Giver*, came just four years after the first winner. Some seeds for this novel were sown during Lois's time as an adolescent in the strange, seemingly perfect American land of Washington Heights, Tokyo, Japan. In this novel the sameness and safety of a manufactured society becomes something ominous rather than comforting. Jonas, who is eleven and turning twelve, is given an honored Assignment: the Receiver of Memory. He will receive and store memories for his community, then experience the pleasure and pain in solitude to spare citizens the burden. He also gains the wisdom and beauty of remembering. Before the Assignment, in his literally colorless world, Jonas first perceives a change in an ordinary apple that he tosses around with his friend Asher. Later he will understand that the change is the color red that flickers briefly but repeatedly across his awareness, on a spectrum denied to his society. The redness of the apple signifies the change that ultimately will interrupt his orderly, monotone existence.

In later years reviewers would note that this novel paved the way for other YA dystopian books such as *The Hunger Games* trilogy, the *Harry Potter* wizard universe, and the *Twilight* vampire franchise. It is also a banned book, ranking twenty-third in the American Library Association's top 100 banned or challenged books between the years 2000 and 2009. Regarding censorship, Lois states that to submit to it is "to enter the seductive world of *The Giver*: the world where there are no bad words and no bad deeds. But it is also the world where choice has been taken away and reality distorted. And that is the most dangerous world of all."

Lois at age 12 in the Washington Heights, Tokyo, Japan, setting that inspired *The Giver*.

Lois with son Grey at his Eagle Scout ceremony in 1973.

Chapter 6
OTHER TRAGIC LOSSES

In 1989 Lois traveled to Europe for a happy occasion: the wedding of her elder son Grey to his German bride, Margret. Their daughter, her granddaughter, Nadine, was born in 1993. Lois's 1998 autobiography, *Looking Back*, features memories and photographs of Nadine sharing story time with her father. Bilingual in German and English, the young child especially enjoyed a certain book about *Schmetterlings*, or butterflies.

Two years after *The Giver* was published, in 1995, Grey was killed in a plane crash. He had been a fighter pilot in the U.S. Air Force during the first Gulf War. Lois says that "his death in the cockpit of a warplane left a little girl fatherless and tore away a piece of my world." During his funeral in Germany, a yellow *Schmetterling* entered the church and flew delicately above the mourners until everyone noticed its special presence.

Years later, Lois's younger son Ben and his wife would name their son Grey in his honor. The pain and pleasure of memories would sustain them through the loss of a son and brother. In her autobiography, *Looking Back*, Lois bridged past and present pain by going "back, and back, and back" to her family in earlier generations and having imagined conversations with her mother, Kate, who had lost a child, her sister Helen, at about the same stage in life.

Many of Lois's plotlines in fact revolve around the subject of loss. *A Summer to Die* focuses on an untimely death that separates young sisters. In *Number the Stars*, Annemarie loses her older sister, Lise, to a deadly accident, and then loses her friend Ellen to the consequences of war. Jonas loses his childhood and sacrifices his comfortable ignorance by choosing to abandon his safe society in *The Giver*.

Following the death of her son, Lois continued her prolific writing endeavors. She wrote her autobiography, then completed two novels in *The Giver* quartet, *Gathering Blue* (2000) and *Messenger* (2004). Harkening back to her passion for photography, Lois wrote *The Silent Boy* in 2003 after she inherited her great aunt's photos from the early twentieth century. An image of a nameless boy in overalls looking as if a story were pent up inside him led her to visit his world.

Then the world of dreams beckoned to Lois in her 2006 novel, *Gossamer*. But this is not a simple tale of fairy dust and lullabies. "Whether we want it to be so or not, our kids have to be able to live in this world," she says. "There will always be a place for bunnies who talk in rhyme, but that's not what I do." Littlest One is in training as a dream-giver when her teacher Thin Elderly agrees to help a disturbed eight-year-old boy who has been abused in the foster care system. Together, Littlest and her teacher work to protect John from their enemy the Sinisteeds, bringers of nightmares. In 2008 Lois adapted the novel into a play for the Oregon Children's Theatre. This group has also done two other adaptations of Lois's books: *The Giver* and *Gathering Blue*. Stan Foote has been the director of the Oregon Children's Theatre. "Stan and I have some plans for future dramatic mischief together," Lois reports on her blog.

Throughout these years Lois enjoyed a long and loving partnership with Martin. They explored the world together but also shared quiet times on the porch doing the *New York Times* crossword puzzle. When Martin died in spring 2011, Lois once again had to open the gate to a different, uncharted world.

Lois with her animal companions, Alfie and Lulu.

Chapter 7
WHAT'S NEXT FOR LOIS?

After Martin's death Lois moved her home base from Cambridge, Massachusetts, to Falmouth, Maine. Downsizing books and treasures while attending book events and creating new fiction was a challenge. She now writes every day with her Tibetan terrier, Alfie, and her cat, Lulu, lounging about, while having grandchildren and friends visit year-round. She maintains her website and updates her blog regularly. Her ambitious travel plans continue, with Tuscany and Cuba on the list for the months ahead.

Lois has made sure that Gooney Bird Greene reprises her second-grade antics, now covering the month of March (published fall 2013), in the series that began in 2002 with October and documenting Gooney Bird's entire school year, month by month.

In 2012 she released *Son*, the conclusion to *The Giver* saga. Gabriel is a teenager and Jonas has a young family. Lois admits that letting go of familiar characters can be difficult. But she insists that there will be no fifth book. *Son* ends with decisive, bold caps: THE END.

When Lois is not busy writing, visiting family, entertaining friends, or traveling to book conferences and vacation spots around the globe, she enjoys knitting, gardening, and keeping up with the goings-on of her beloved family, friends, and pets. She's an enthusiastic cook and has an enormous cookbook collection. She hosts Super Bowl parties and watches the New England Patriots and the Boston Red Sox play throughout their seasons.

As a gifted photographer who studied the art in graduate school, her work has been featured on the covers of her two Newbery Medal-winners. She photographed and knew personally both the old man on the cover of *The Giver* and the young girl on the cover of *Number the Stars*. In her early writing career, Lois was also a professional child photographer. Nowadays she is as likely to hand a camera to visiting grandchildren and to admire the photos they take around her home and property.

Life is full and good for Lois Lowry, as she writes "back, and back, and back" into her experiences and memories, always discovering new pathways into the "Elsewhere" we both fear and long for, no matter how old or young we may be.

THE GIVER: SOON AT YOUR LOCAL MULTIPLEX?

Plans to film Lois's groundbreaking book have been circulating in Hollywood for years. Yet the author has her doubts about whether the world of Jonas can ever be conveyed on the big screen. "It's a book with not a lot of action. And it's largely introspective." Oscar winner Jeff Bridges bought the film rights originally, as a vehicle for the Giver character to be played by his father, celebrated actor Lloyd Bridges. But Lloyd passed away in 1998 and son Jeff actually is now old enough to step into the role himself. The search continues for the young actor who would play Jonas. "I think what they should do is hold a national search," Lois says. "Because kids across the country know the book, and they would be very excited by that. And that's how they could find the right boy for the part. But who knows what they have in mind."

Actor Jeff Bridges wants to produce a film based on *The Giver*.

At age 7, Lois's granddaughter, Nadine, already loved to read.

LOIS LIKES TO READ

Lois is an enthusiastic reader and always has a stack of books written by other authors, waiting for her attention once she has time off from writing her own books. The stories that have influenced her the most are those that "combine a profound knowledge of childhood with a masterful gift for language."

These are the books she considers indispensable companions on her journey as a writer and a reader:

A Death in the Family by James Agee

Cat's Eye by Margaret Atwood

The Handmaid's Tale by Margaret Atwood

The Secret Garden by Frances Hodgson Burnett

James and the Giant Peach by Roald Dahl

The Unlikely Pilgrimage of Harold Fry by Rachel Joyce

To Kill a Mockingbird by Harper Lee

So Long, See You Tomorrow by William Maxwell

The Yearling by Marjorie Kinnan Rawlings

A Tree Grows in Brooklyn by Betty Smith

The Collected Short Stories by William Trevor

The Collected Letters of E.B. White

BOOKS BY LOIS LOWRY

THE QUARTET

The Giver (1993)

Gathering Blue (2000)

Messenger (2004)

Son (2012)

ANASTASIA KRUPNIK SERIES

Anastasia Krupnik (1979)

Anastasia Again! (1981)

Anastasia at Your Service (1982)

Anastasia Ask Your Analyst (1984)

Anastasia on Her Own (1985)

Anastasia Has the Answers (1986)

Anastasia's Chosen Career (1987)

Anastasia at This Address (1991)

Anastasia Absolutely (1995)

SAM KRUPNIK SERIES

All About Sam (1988)

Attaboy Sam! (1992)

See You Around, Sam! (1996)

Zooman Sam (1999)

TATE FAMILY

The One Hundredth Thing About Caroline (1983)

Switcharound (1985)

Your Move, J.P.! (1990)

GOONEY BIRD

Gooney Bird Greene (2002)

Gooney Bird and the Room Mother (2006)

Gooney the Fabulous (2007)

Gooney Bird Is So Absurd (2009)

Gooney Bird on the Map (2011)

Gooney Bird and All Her Charms (2013)

AUTOBIOGRAPHY

Looking Back (1998)

STAND-ALONE TITLES

A Summer to Die (1977)

Here in Kennebunkport (1978)

Find a Stranger, Say Goodbye (1978)

Autumn Street (1980)

Taking Care of Terrific (1983)

Us and Uncle Fraud (1984)

Rabble Starkey (1987)

Number the Stars (1989)

Stay! Keeper's Story (1997)

The Silent Boy (2003)

Gossamer (2006)

The Willoughbys (2008)

Crow Call (2009)

The Birthday Ball (2010)

Bless This Mouse (2011)

Like the Willow Tree (*Dear America* series) (2011)

The Chronicles of Harris Burdick by Chris Van Allsburg (2011),
    contributing author

GLOSSARY

bequeathed—handed down or passed on, as in money or property, by a will

bilingual—able to speak two languages well, especially as a native speaker of both

cherubic—angelic, childlike, innocent

cusp—a point marking the beginning of a change

dystopian—having to do with a society in which values and trends lead to a lessened quality of life

franchise—a right granted by a corporation or a government to a person or a group of individuals; specifically, to a series of books or films to sell or use products

homogenous—of the same kind or nature; basically alike

hopscotched—jumped or leaped from one place to another, quickly and directly

introspective—to examine one's own mind or feelings

monotone—a uniformed tone of one color; sameness

ominous—suggesting an evil or serious consequence

precocious—unusually mature or advanced in talent or intellectual development

pungent—having a powerful smell or taste

rambunctious—noisy and active

CHRONOLOGY

March 20, 1937: Lois Ann Hammersberg is born in Honolulu, Hawaii.

1939: The Hammersberg family moves to Brooklyn, New York.

1942: Lois's father serves in World War II; the family moves to Carlisle, PA.

1948: The family moves to Japan.

1950: Lois, her mother, and siblings move back to Carlisle. Their father remains in Japan.

1951: The Hammersbergs move to Governors Island, New York City.

1954-1956: Lois attends Brown University in Rhode Island; she leaves in 1956 to marry Donald Lowry.

1958: Daughter Alix is born.

1959: Son Grey is born.

1961: Daughter Kristin is born.

1962: Lois's sister Helen dies of cancer; son Benjamin is born.

1963: The Lowry family moves to Maine.

1972: Lois earns a B.A. from the University of Southern Maine.

1977: The Lowrys are divorced, Lois's first novel, *A Summer to Die*, is published.

1979: Lois moves to Boston, Massachusetts.

1990: *Number the Stars* is awarded the Newbery Medal.

1994: *The Giver* is awarded the Newbery Medal.

1995: Grey Lowry is killed in a plane crash.

2000: *Gathering Blue* is published.

2004: *Messenger* is published.

2011: Lois's partner of thirty years, Martin, passes away.

2012: *Son* is published, completing the *Giver* quartet.

2013: *Gooney Bird and All Her Charms* is published.

FURTHER
INFORMATION

Books

Are you interested in trying to write stories yourself? These two books offer guidance.

Levine, Gail Carson. *Writing Magic: Creating Stories that Fly*. New York: Collins, 2006.

Messner, Kate. *Real Revision: Authors' Strategies to Share with Student Writers*. Portland, OR: Stenhouse, 2011.

Websites

Lois's Website:

www.loislowry.com

Lois Lowry: BookPage

www.bookpage.com/author/lois-lowry

Lois Lowry: The Giver Quartet

www.hmhbooks.com/thegiverquartet/index.html

"Lois Lowry Interview: Part 1." Writer Unboxed. http://writerunboxed. com/2007/04/20/interview-lois-lowry-part-1/

"Lois Lowry Interview: Part 2." Writer Unboxed. http://writerunboxed. com/2007/04/27/interview-lois-lowry-part-2/

Lois Lowry Interview: www.indiebound.org/author-interviews/lowry

Online Video/Audio

Radio Boston: Author Lois Lowry on Her Work and Life.
http://radioboston.wbur.org/2013/01/07/lois-lowry

Reading Rockets Children's Books and Authors: Lois Lowry
http://www.readingrockets.org/books/interviews/lowry/

"*The Giver* author describes upcoming fourth book; movie in the works." Studio 360 www.pri.org/stories/arts-entertainment/books/the-giver-author-describes-upcoming-fourth-book-movie-in-the-works-12576.html

BIBLIOGRAPHY

A note to report writers

To write this biography, I read several of Lois's books and did research online that included reading articles written about Lois by other journalists. I also contacted Lois to get the latest news on her travels and book projects. Below is a list of sources I used. Any time you write a report, you should also keep track of your sources for information. It is fine to use information in your report that you found somewhere else, as long as you give the source credit in a footnote, endnote, or within the report itself. (Your teacher can tell you how he or she prefers you list your sources.)

It is not fine to pass off other people's work as your own.

PRINT ARTICLES

Busis, Hillary. "Lois Lowry Returns to 'The Giver.'" *Entertainment Weekly*, November 2, 2012.

Corbett, Sue. "Children's Bookshelf Talks with Lois Lowry." *Publishers Weekly*, January 24, 2008.

Griffin, Lynn, R.N., M.Ed. "Born In-Between: The Secret Power of Middle Children." *Psychology Today*, October 18, 2012.

Kois, Dan. "The Children's Author Who Actually Listens to Children." *New York Times*, October 3, 2012.

Lodge, Sally. "Lois Lowry: Snapshots from Her Life." *Publishers Weekly*, September 7, 1998.

ONLINE SOURCES

Hughley, Marty, "'Gossamer': A Play So Good It's Dreamy," *The Oregonian*, October 16, 2008, www.oregonlive.com/performance/index. ssf/2008/10/gossamer_a_play_so_good_its_dr.html

Hynes, James, "Dream Weavers," review of *Gossamer* by Lois Lowry, *New York Times*, May 14, 2006, Sunday Book Review, www.nytimes. com/2006/05/14/books/review/14hynes.html

"Lois Lowry Biography," Amazon, http://www.amazon.com/Lois-Lowry/e/B000AP6Y8C

Wasserman, Robin, "The Searcher," review of *Son* by Lois Lowry, *New York Times*, October 11, 2012, Sunday Book Review, www.nytimes. com/2012/10/14/books/review/son-by-lois-lowry.html

INDEX

ABOUT THE AUTHOR:

Deborah Grahame-Smith is a writer and editor who has worked for children's book publishers including Scholastic, Millbrook Press, and Marshall Cavendish. She is also the author of several nonfiction books for kids. A native of Long Island, New York, she currently lives in Connecticut.